School
Around the World

Kelly Doudna

Consulting Editor, Diane Craig, M.A./Reading Specialist

Published by ABDO Publishing Company, 8000 West 78th Street, Edina, Minnesota 55439.

Printed in the United States of America, North Mankato, Minnesota.
012004   102010
Credits
Edited by: Pam Price
Curriculum Coordinator: Nancy Tuminelly
Cover and Interior Design and Production: Mighty Media
Photo Credits: Corbis Images, Eyewire Images, PhotoDisc, Stockbyte

Library of Congress Cataloging-in-Publication Data

Doudna, Kelly, 1963-
    School around the world / Kelly Doudna.
        p. cm. -- (Around the world)
    Includes index.
    Summary: Describes how schools differ around the world.
    ISBN 1-59197-569-7
        1. Schools--Juvenile literature. 2. Students--Juvenile literature. [1. Schools.] I. Title.

LB1513.D68 2004
371--dc22

2003058395

SandCastle™ books are created by a professional team of educators, reading specialists, and content developers around five essential components that include phonemic awareness, phonics, vocabulary, text comprehension, and fluency. All books are written, reviewed, and leveled for guided reading, early intervention reading, and Accelerated Reader® programs and designed for use in shared, guided, and independent reading and writing activities to support a balanced approach to literacy instruction.

Let Us Know

After reading the book, SandCastle would like you to tell us your stories about reading. What is your favorite page? Was there something hard that you needed help with? Share the ups and downs of learning to read. We want to hear from you! To get posted on the ABDO Publishing Company Web site, send us e-mail at:

sandcastle@abdopub.com

SandCastle Level: Fluent

Schools around the
world have different
ways of doing things.

Understanding and accepting these differences is important.

It makes the world a more peaceful place to live.

Alex and his classmates live in Greece.

They have to go to school only until they are 14 years old.

Nara lives in Japan.

Students wear different uniforms for summer and winter.

They switch in June and October.

Ali and his classmates live in Tanzania.

Class is held outside.

Many towns in Tanzania have no school building.

Liz and Dave live in the United States.

They attend a public school for free.

Tia lives in Mexico.

She has a school holiday on September 16.

That is Independence Day in Mexico.

Kylie and her classmates live in Australia.

Their summer break is in December and January.

What things about your school are different from other schools?

Did You Know?

Australia is in the Southern Hemisphere, so its summer begins in December and its winter begins in June.

Koromogae means "seasonal changing of clothes." Today it refers to June 1 and October 1, when Japanese school children change their uniforms.

In Mexico students have November 2 off from classes to celebrate *Día de los Muertos*, a two-day holiday honoring the dead.

Glossary

accept. to think of as normal, right, or unavoidable

attend. to be present at

break. time off from work, school, or duty

classmate. someone you go to school with

different. not alike

holiday. a day free from school or work, often to celebrate a certain occasion

peaceful. calm, free from disagreement

public. open to all people in a community

uniform. special clothes worn by all members of a group

About SandCastle™

A professional team of educators, reading specialists, and content developers created the SandCastle™ series to support young readers as they develop reading skills and strategies and increase their general knowledge. The SandCastle™ series has four levels that correspond to early literacy development in young children. The levels are provided to help teachers and parents select the appropriate books for young readers.

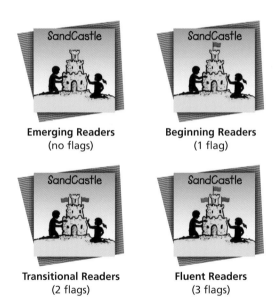

Emerging Readers
(no flags)

Beginning Readers
(1 flag)

Transitional Readers
(2 flags)

Fluent Readers
(3 flags)

These levels are meant only as a guide. All levels are subject to change.

To see a complete list of SandCastle™ books and other nonfiction titles from ABDO Publishing Company, visit www.abdopublishing.com or contact us at:

8000 West 78th Street, Edina, Minnesota 55439 • 1-800-800-1312 • fax: 1-952-831-1632